I0813281

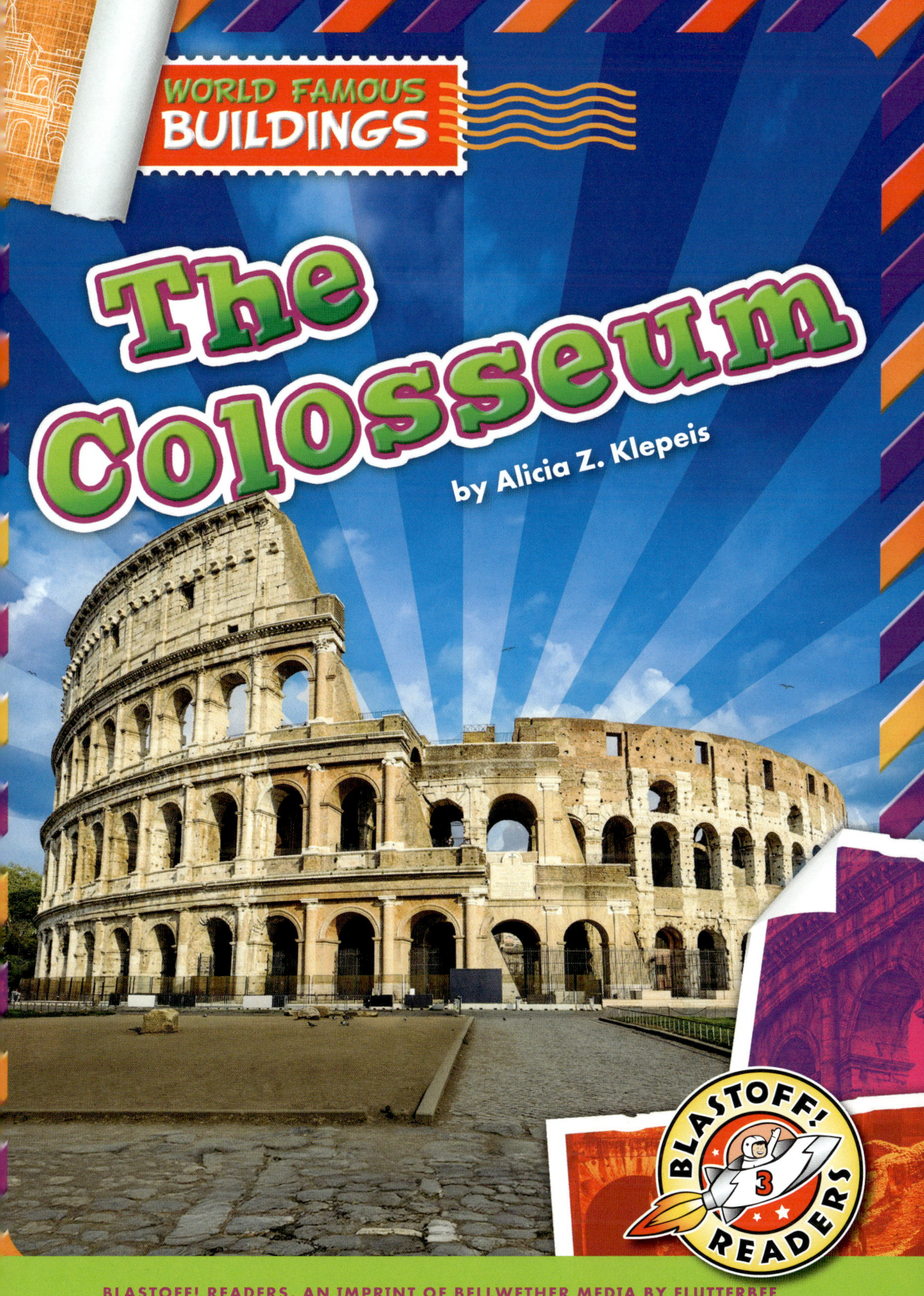


BLASTOFF! READERS, AN IMPRINT OF BELLWETHER MEDIA BY FLUTTERBEE

**Blastoff! Readers** are carefully developed by literacy experts to build reading stamina and move students toward fluency by combining standards-based content with developmentally appropriate text.

**Level 1** provides the most support through repetition of high-frequency words, light text, predictable sentence patterns, and strong visual support.

**Level 2** offers early readers a bit more challenge through varied sentences, increased text load, and text-supportive special features.

**Level 3** advances early-fluent readers toward fluency through increased text load, less reliance on photos, advancing concepts, longer sentences, and more complex special features.

★ **Blastoff! Universe**

Reading Level

Grade K

Grades 1–3

Grade 4

This edition first published in 2026 by Bellwether Media, Inc.



For information regarding permission, write to Bellwether Media, Inc., Attention: Permissions Department, 3500 American Blvd W, Suite 150, Bloomington, MN 55431.

Library of Congress Cataloging-in-Publication Data is available at www.loc.gov or upon request from the publisher.

ISBN: 9798893048056 (hardcover)
ISBN: 9798893049053 (ebook)

Editor: Betsy Rathburn Designer: Laura Sowers

Printed in the United States of America, North Mankato, MN.

# Table of Contents

# What Is the Colosseum?

The Colosseum is a famous building in Italy. It stands in the historic center of Rome.

It is the world's biggest **amphitheater**.

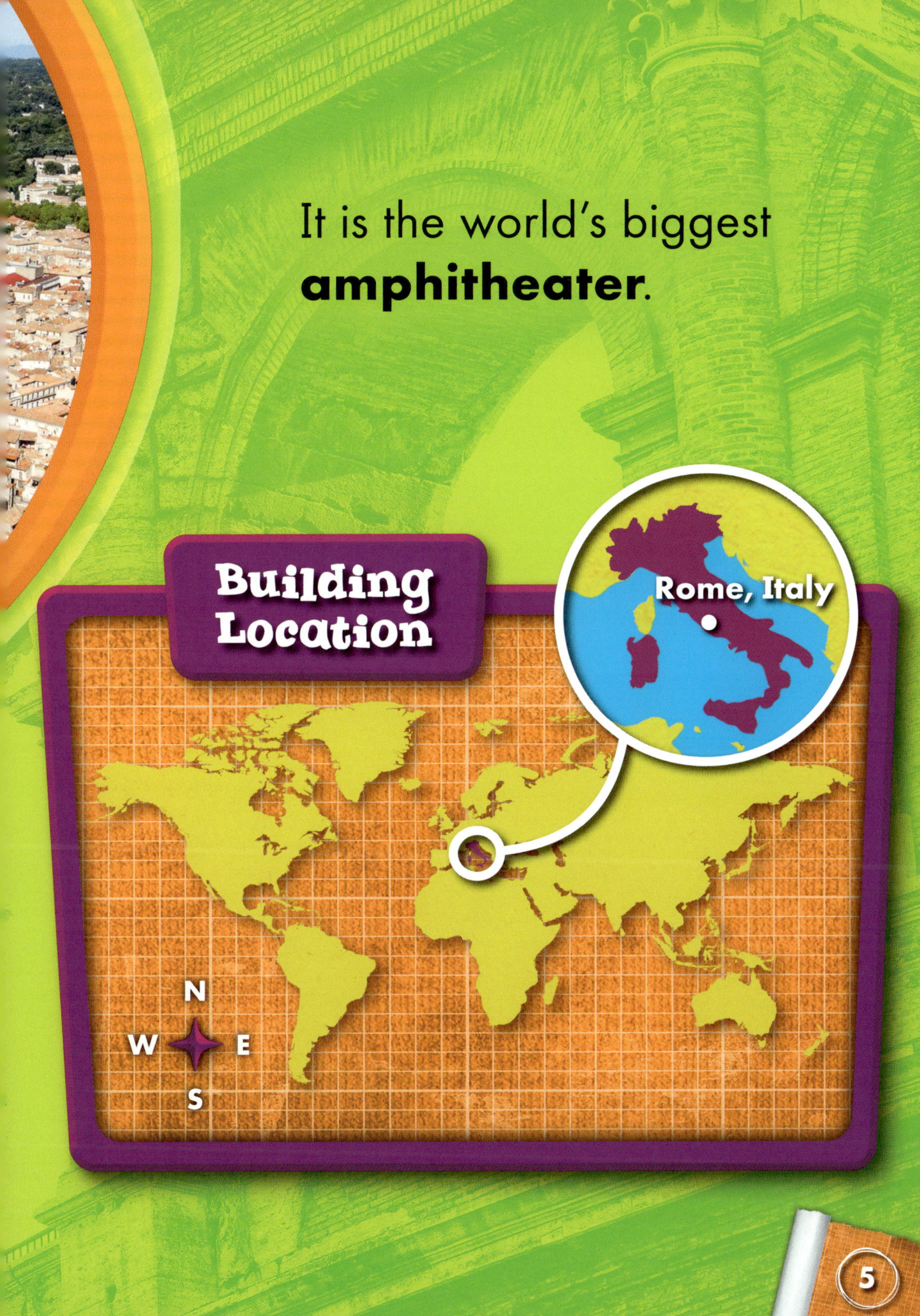

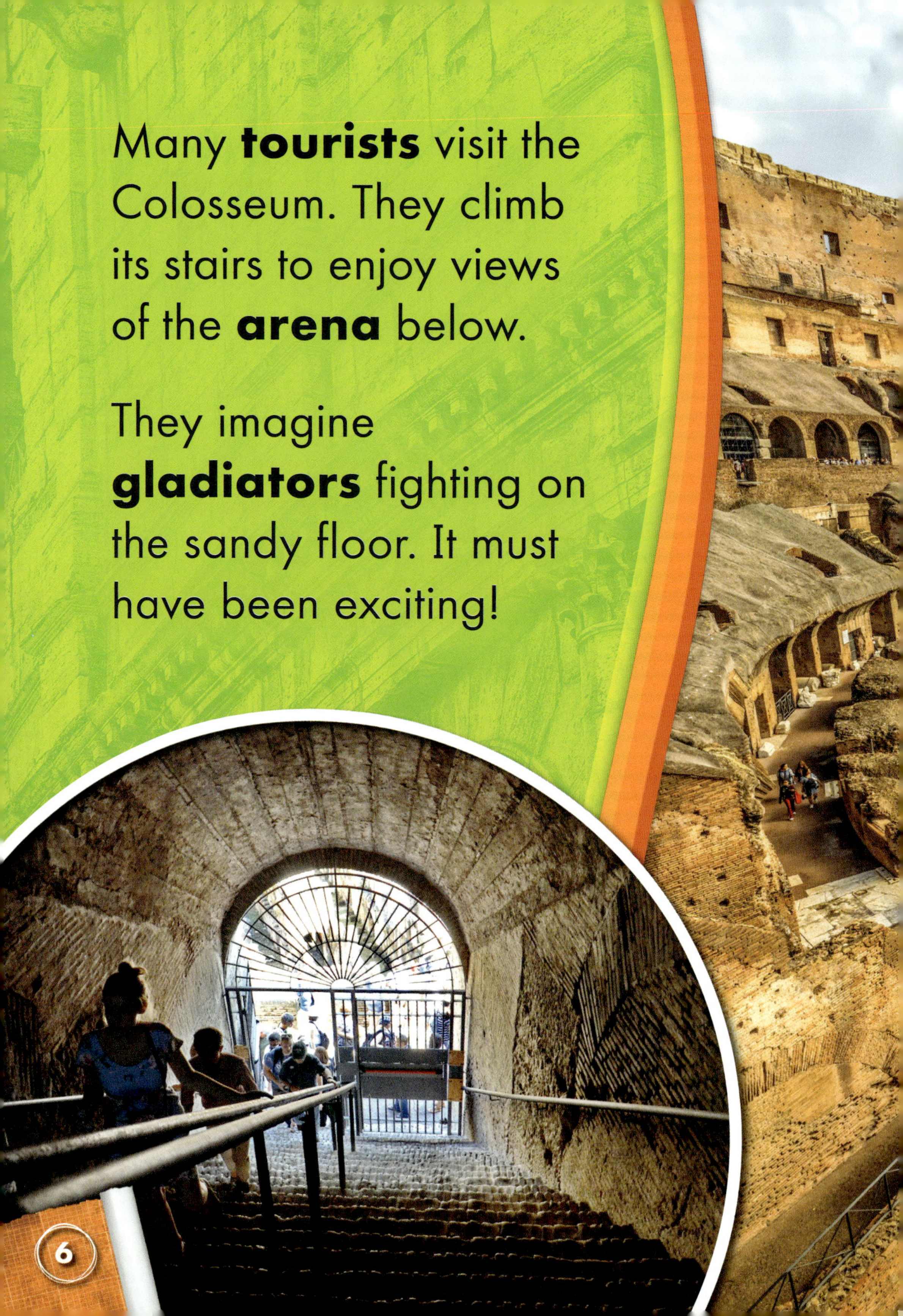

Many **tourists** visit the Colosseum. They climb its stairs to enjoy views of the **arena** below.

They imagine **gladiators** fighting on the sandy floor. It must have been exciting!

arena

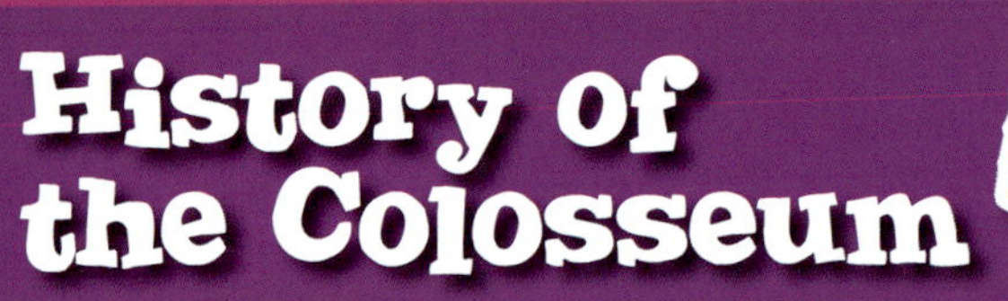

# History of the Colosseum

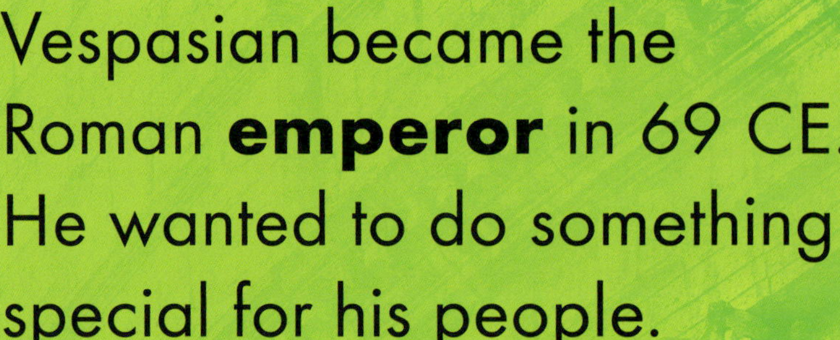

Vespasian became the Roman **emperor** in 69 CE. He wanted to do something special for his people.

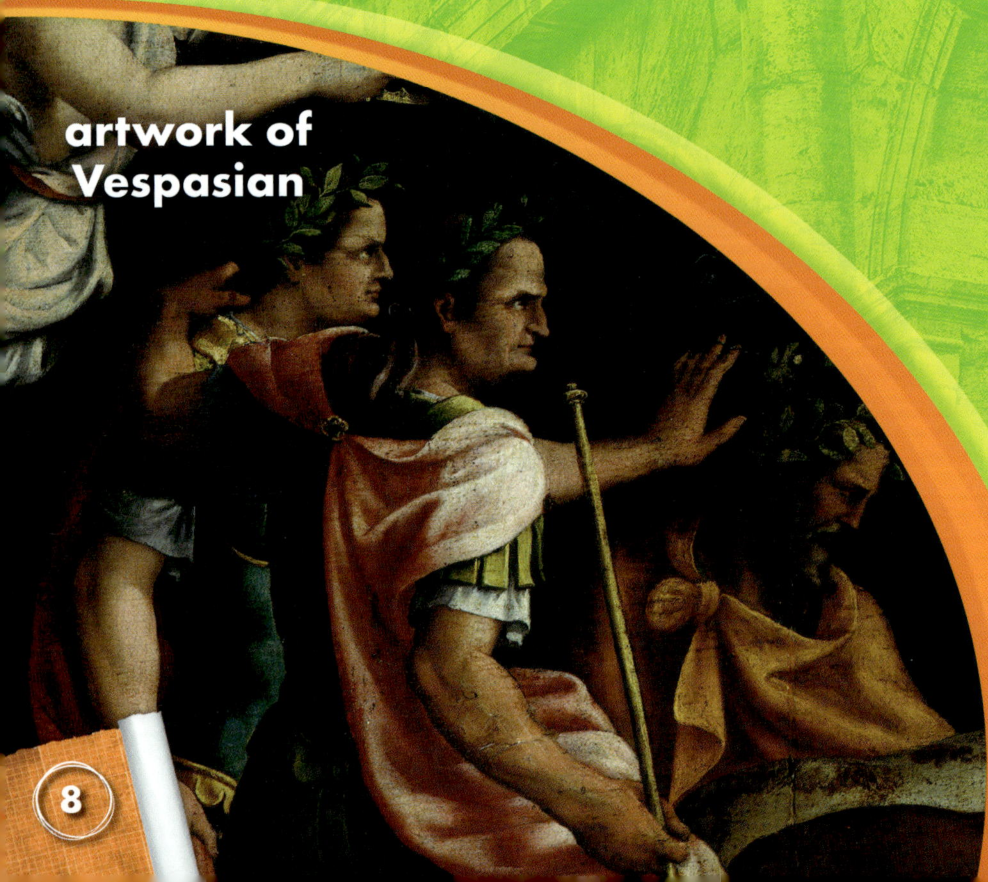

artwork of Vespasian

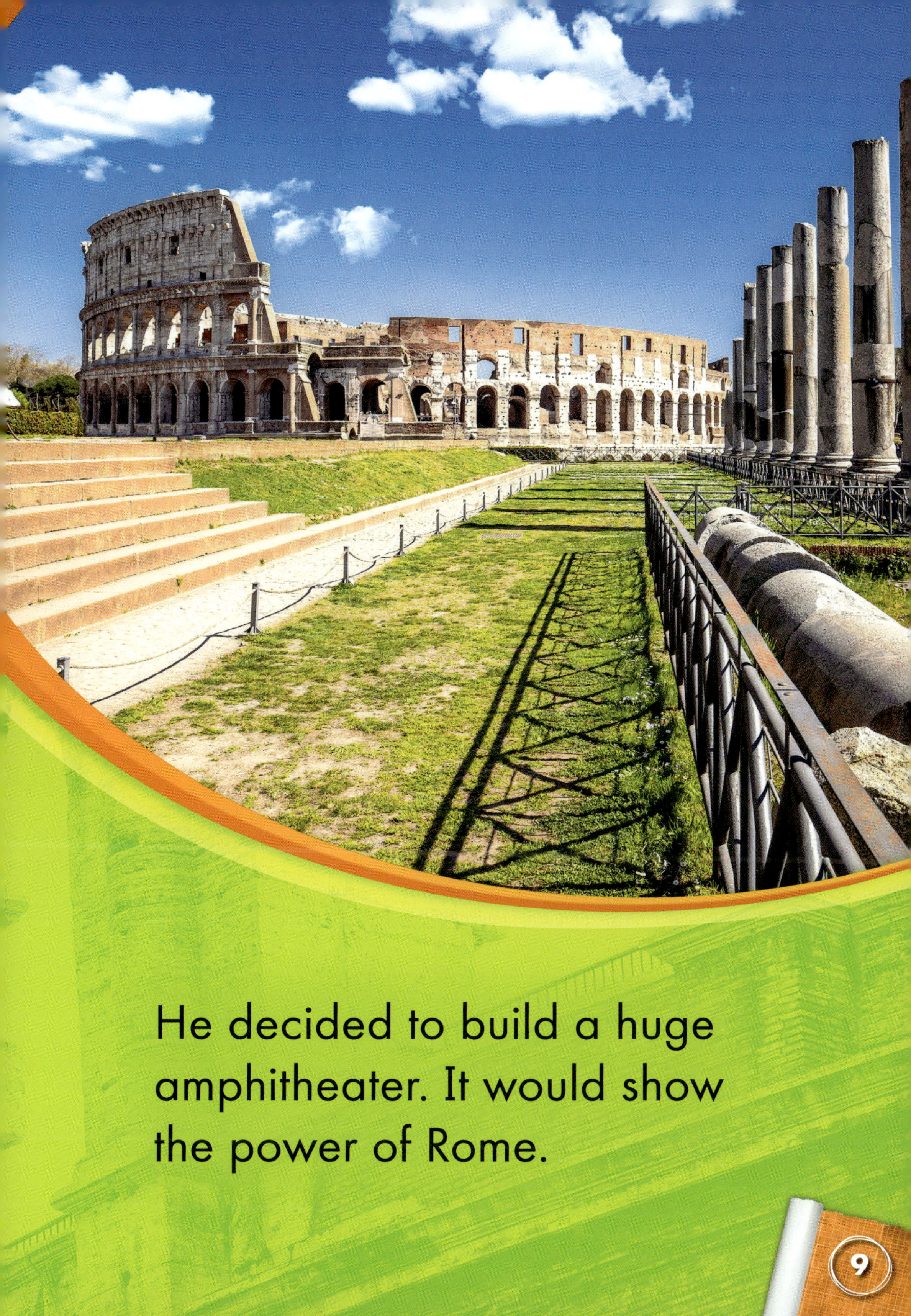

He decided to build a huge amphitheater. It would show the power of Rome.

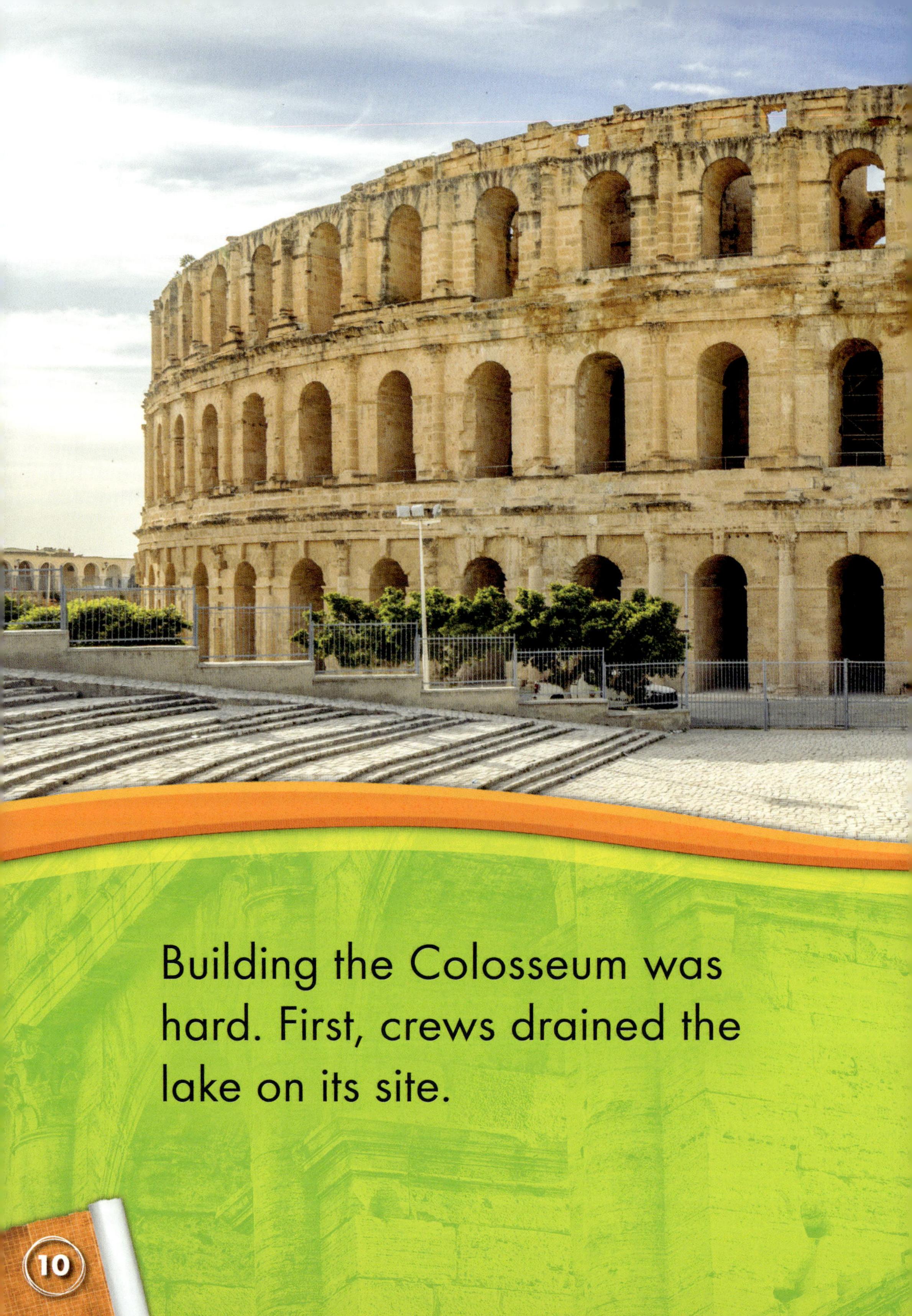

Building the Colosseum was hard. First, crews drained the lake on its site.

Next, they laid the **foundation**. It was made of concrete. It had a donut shape. This material and shape helped support the building.

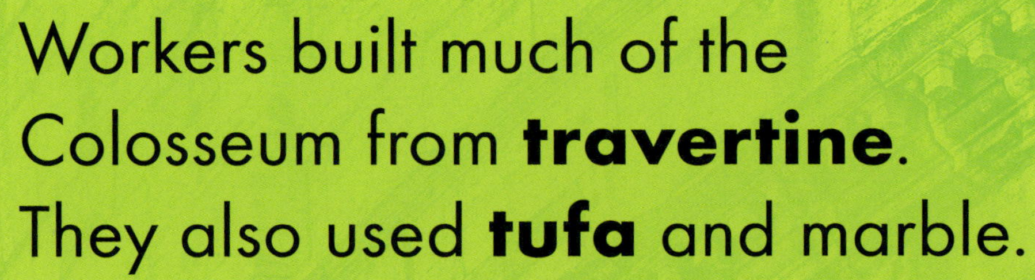

Workers built much of the Colosseum from **travertine**. They also used **tufa** and marble.

The building opened in 80 CE. There were 100 days of games to celebrate. People hunted wild animals. There were even **mock** sea battles!

# Parts of the Colosseum

The Colosseum is famous for its arches. They make up the lower **facade**. There are 240 in all!

Columns frame the arches. Each level has a different column style. The fourth and fifth levels were added later.

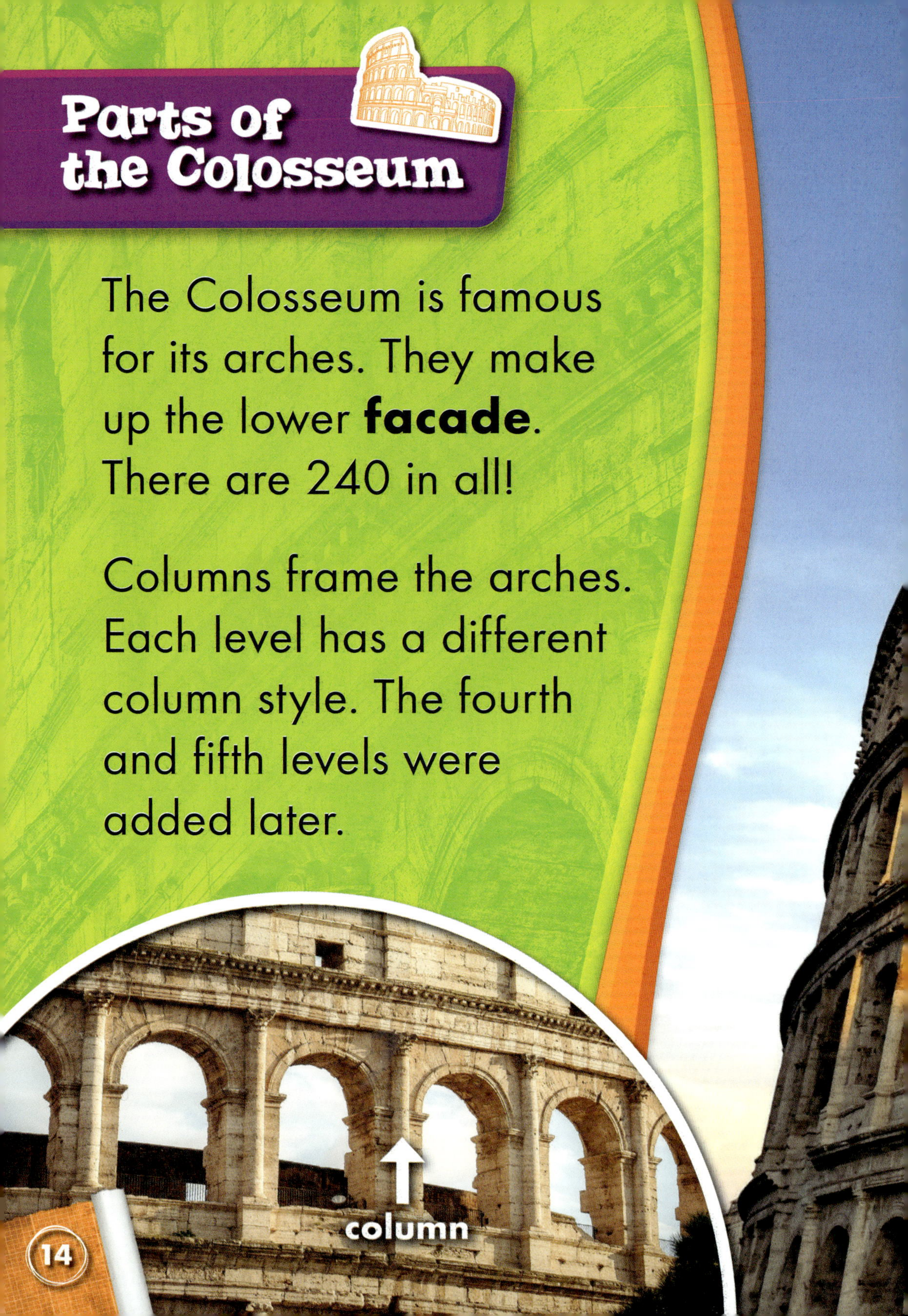

Awesome Arches
What They Are Made Of
a group of wedge-shaped blocks forming a semicircle
What They Do
support heavy upper levels
arch
lower facade

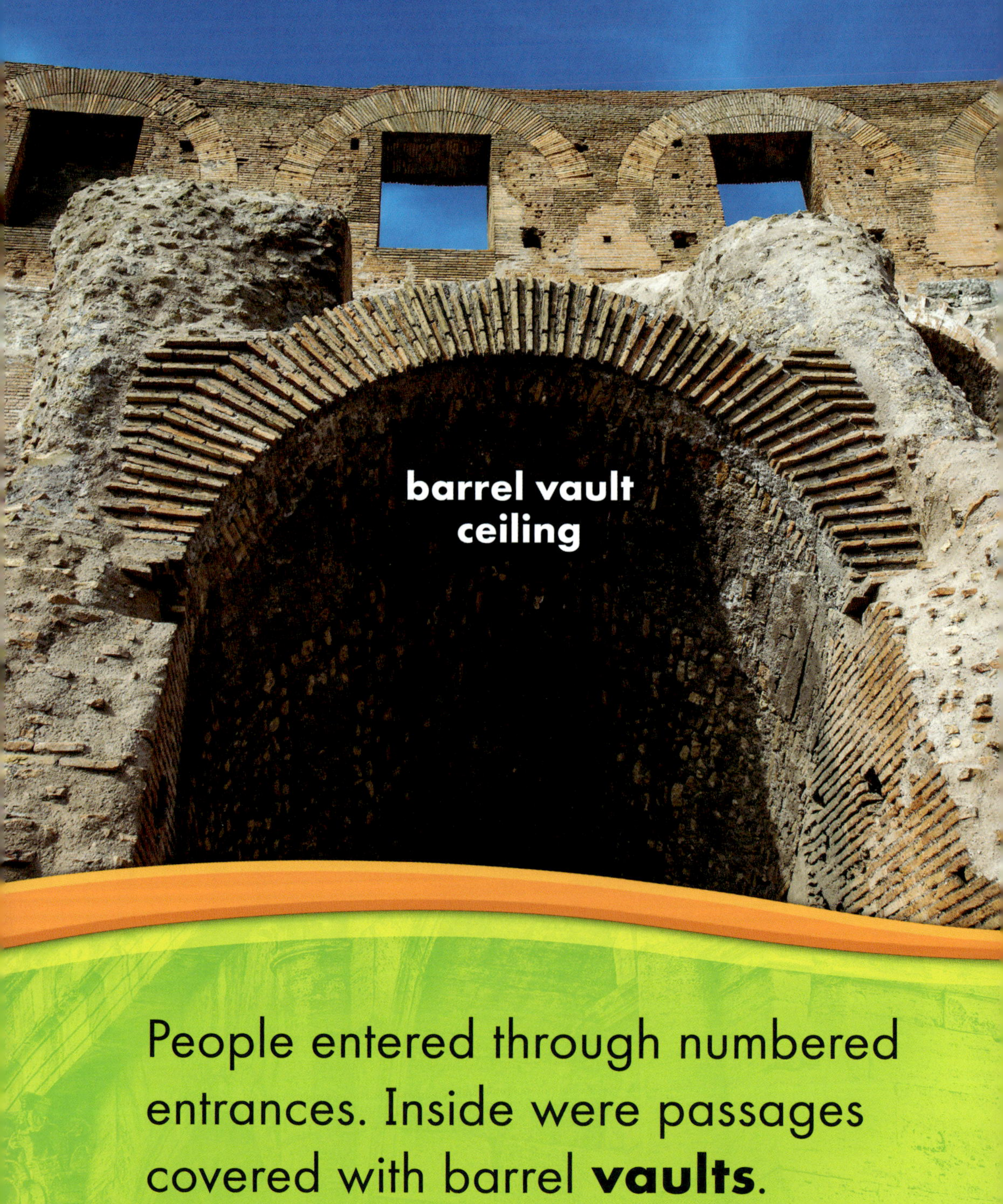


People entered through numbered entrances. Inside were passages covered with barrel **vaults**. Rows of seats stretched high up.

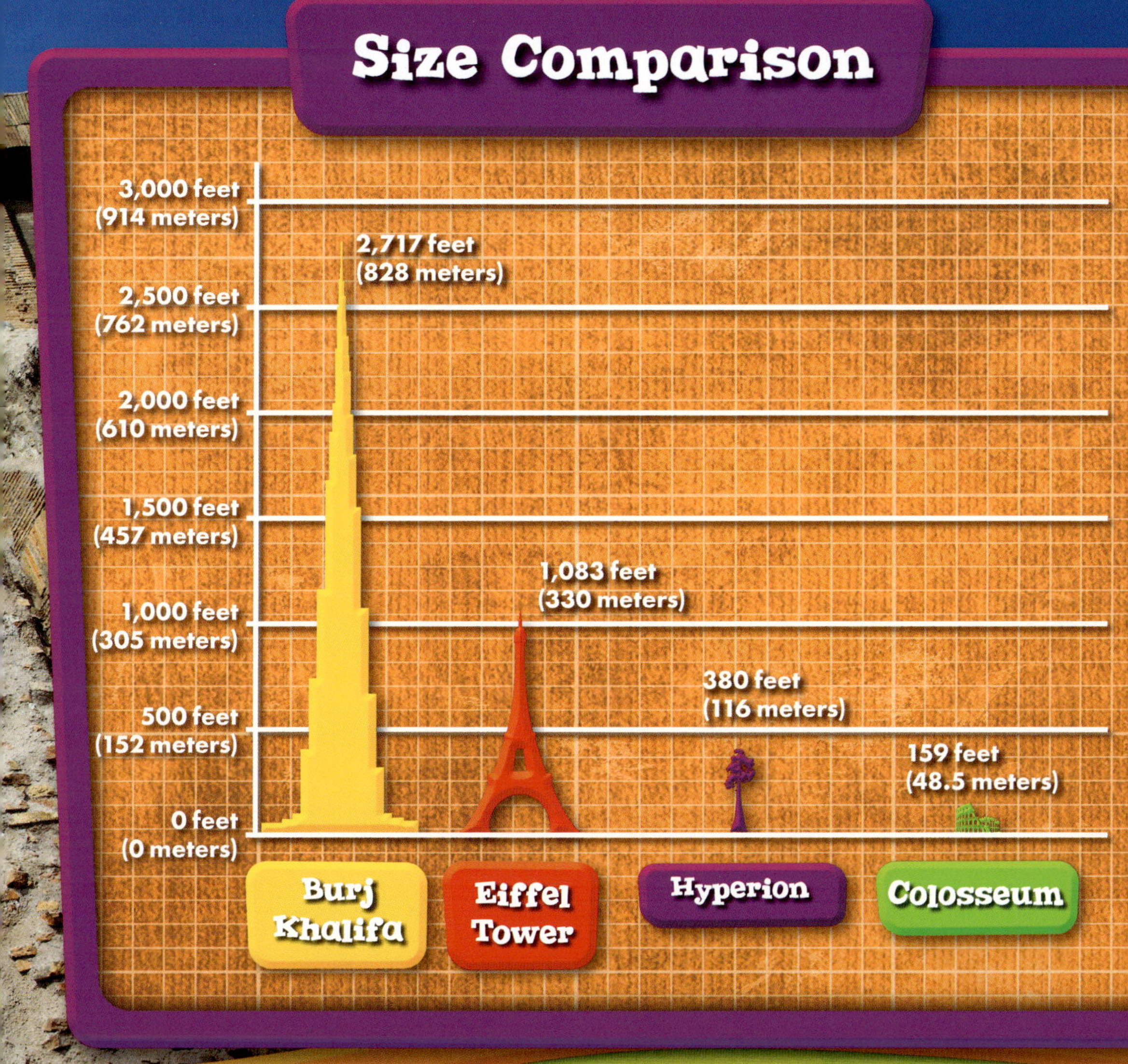


The arena could hold up to 80,000 people. A huge **awning** offered shade on sunny days.

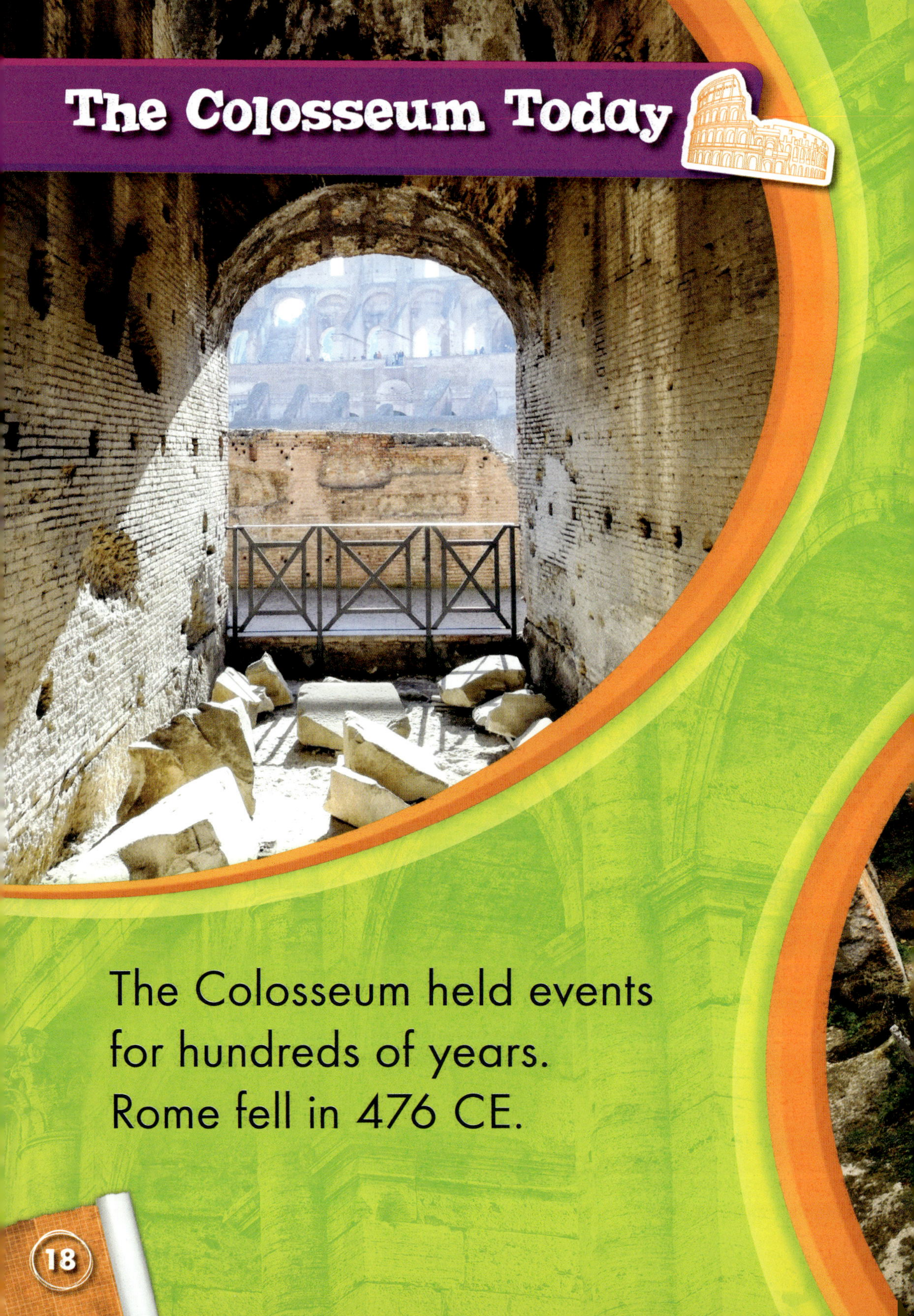

# The Colosseum Today

The Colosseum held events for hundreds of years. Rome fell in 476 CE.

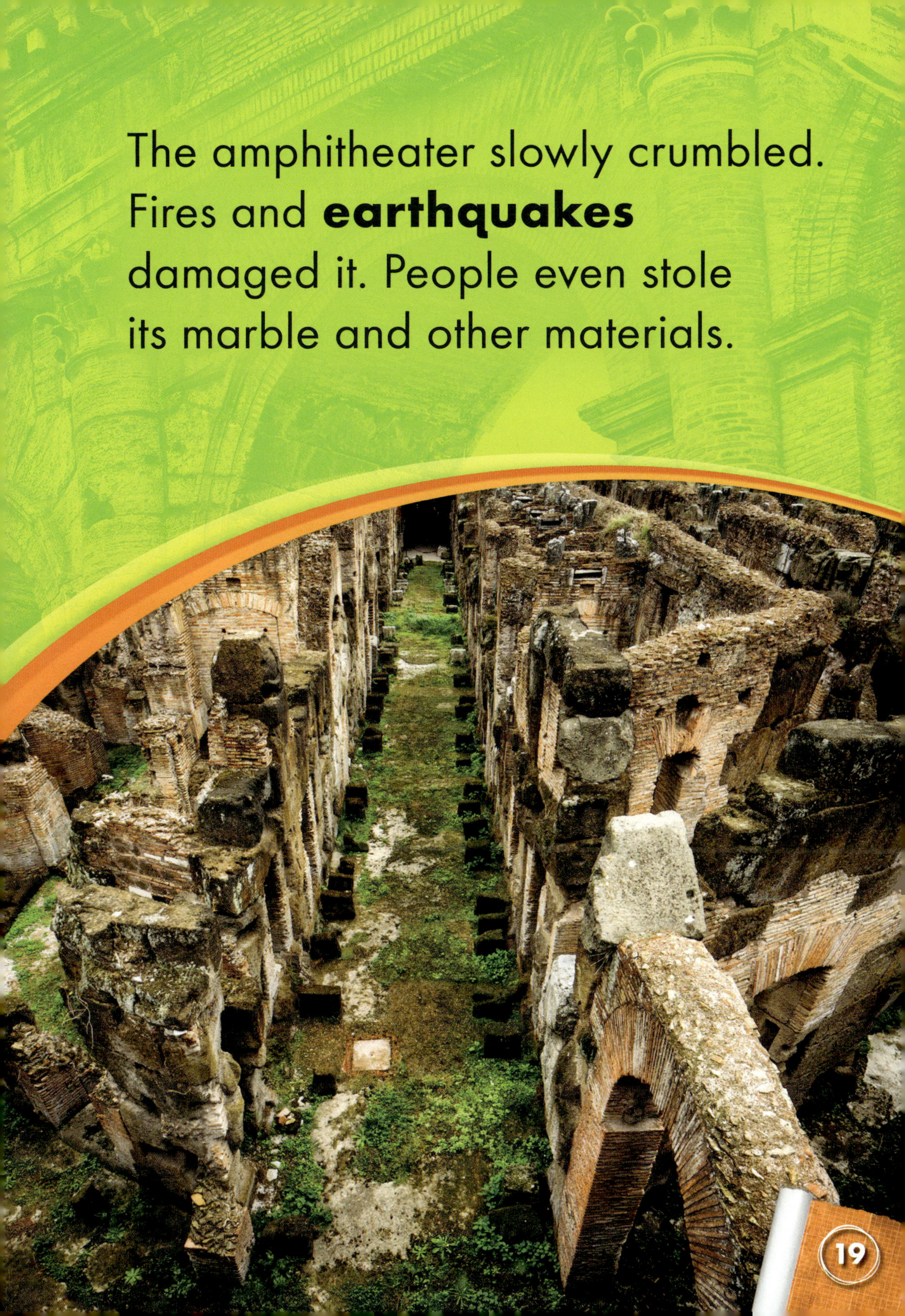

The amphitheater slowly crumbled. Fires and **earthquakes** damaged it. People even stole its marble and other materials.

Serious efforts to fix the landmark began in the 1990s. Workers cleaned its walls. They repaired its stonework. They started rebuilding its floor.

This famous building gets over six million visitors each year!

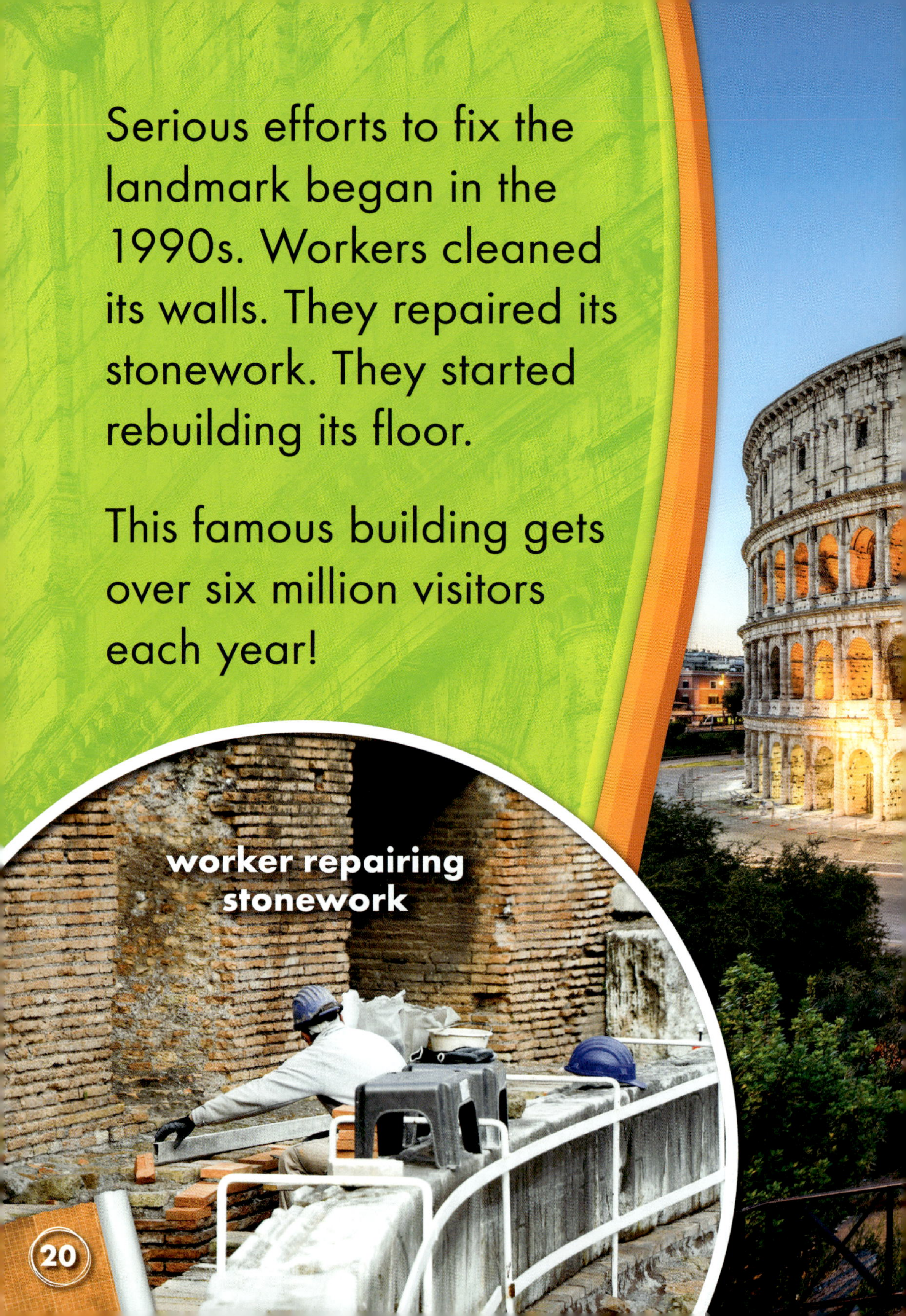

worker repairing stonework

# Glossary

**amphitheater**—an oval or round building with levels of seats that rise from a central area

**arena**—a big area surrounded by seats often used for sports, music, or other events

**awning**—a cloth roof

**earthquakes**—sudden movements of the earth's crust

**emperor**—ruler

**facade**—the front of a building

**foundation**—the base or support on which a building rests

**gladiators**—people who fought other people or animals, often to their death, to entertain ancient Romans

**mock**—not real

**tourists**—people who travel to visit another place

**travertine**—a type of light-colored limestone used as a building material

**tufa**—a soft rock with a spongelike texture

**vaults**—arched structures made of stonework that typically form ceilings or roofs

# To Learn More

## AT THE LIBRARY

Jopp, Kelsey. *Colosseum.* Lake Elmo, Minn.: Focus Readers, 2023.

Simons, Lisa M. Bolt. *Colosseum.* Mankato, Minn.: Creative Education, 2025.

Spanier, Kristine. *Colosseum.* Minneapolis, Minn.: Jump!, 2021.

## ON THE WEB

**FACTSURFER**

Factsurfer.com gives you a safe, fun way to find more information.

1. Go to www.factsurfer.com.
2. Enter "Colosseum" into the search box and click 🔍.
3. Select your book cover to see a list of related content.

# Index



The images in this book are reproduced through the courtesy of: Mapics, front cover; Klicker, front cover (inset 1); Andrea Izzotti, front cover (inset 2); Aleksey Arkhipov, p. 3; saiko3p, pp. 4-5; Bob Hilscher, p. 6; Old Town Tourist, pp. 6-7; DEA/ G. DAGLI ORTI/ Contributor/ Getty Images, p. 8; xbrchx, pp. 8-9; Vadim_N, pp. 10-11; givaga, p. 12, 13 (concrete); LifeCollectionPhotography, p. 13 (travertine); In Case You're Wondering, p. 13 (tufa); AlfvanBeem/ Wikipedia, p. 13 (marble); Photocreo Bednarek, p. 13; NorthSky Films, p. 14; Anaglacourt, pp. 14-15; Eslam, p. 15; anamejia18, pp. 16-17; Gillian Tapping, p. 18; Viacheslav Lopatin, pp. 18-19; Simona Balconi, p. 20; mapman, pp. 20-21; Miso Ai, p. 23.